RAISING LEADERS IN THE CLASSROOM

A STUDENT-TEACHER HANDBOOK

HEATHER THANE

Copyright © 2014 Heather Thane
All rights reserved.

No portion of this book may be reproduced, stored in a retrieval system or transmitted in any form or by any means – electronic, mechanical, photocopy, recording, or other – except for brief quotations in printed reviews, without prior permission from the publisher.

www.greatnesspublishing.org

Cover Design and formatting by Farouk J. Roberts,
Brands & Love Creative
www.brandsnlove.com

Library and Archives Canada
ISBN 978-1-927579-12-1

Other Books by Heather Thane

"Unlock your Greatness Leadership Coaches' Manual"

This accompanying manual is an invaluable resource tool. It appeals not just to the intellect but to the heart of the emotions and the will upon which everything depends. It contains helpful activities for reflective thinking and for guiding the thought in the decision making process. The lessons contained herein are so designed to involve and engage students to facilitate discovery learning. The strategic questions asked and the suggested activities capitalize on the different levels of higher order learning. Students cannot help but get the right impression that using their potential and abilities aright; they can make a positive contribution to the solution of the world's problems.

"I am a Leader Coaches' Manual"

This manual is punctuated with very practical and helpful strategies in implementing its counterpart handbook text. Its holistic approach leads the mind of the student along a path that is designed to bring about a transforming experience. It has the potential of making a great inspirational impact on teachers. It aims at developing the skills and boosting the motivations as well as clarifying the approach teachers and coaches needs to be successful in their roles as change agents in the field of education.

Clear attainable goals and practical step by step directions are delineated in almost every page. This text clarifies the role of leadership in a manner easily understood with clear, simple, relevant examples and illustrations. It will most certainly give purposeful, enjoyable meaning and implementation to the teacher.

Saul Leacock BSc (SW), M.Ed (Psy).
President, Barbados Association of Guidance Counsellors

"Teaching Educators to Raise Leaders: 3D Leadership Concept"

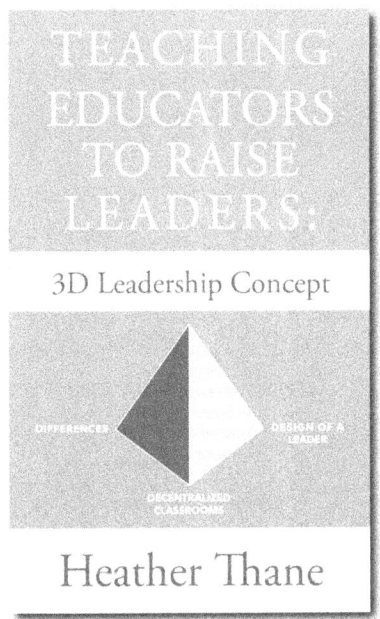

POEM
STRIVE FOR MASTERY

September is over
The thrill of new faces and fresh starts are in the past
The new teacher is alone in the classroom
Consumed with learning the names
Identifying the learning styles
Of the many individuals
Placed in care

Schedules are released
Requiring attendance
At Workshops, Staff Training, Parent Meetings
All of such
While adjusting to every area of daily work

As new teachers strive for mastery
Having a good beginning
Makes it more likely to thrive
Remembering Teachers are Leaders
And Need to be given the freedom
To stretch themselves
To make mistakes and try again
To fulfill their potential
Free of any bias

By Heather Thane

Acknowledgments

This book would not have been possible without skillful brainstorming ideas and thoughts from persons who read and endorsed some of my other titles.

Special thanks to my colleagues, Justine Palcich, and Angie Fehr for their thoughtful comments on the topic.

Thanks too, to Paulette McTaggart, who has so skillfully edited my book.

I would also wish to thank Eric McDonald and Algie Williams for sending me frequent notes to say "Keep up the good work" and reminding me of my goal to touch the lives of millions of people.

Thanks to Greatness Publishing and Farouk Roberts for adding graphic expertise to my book.

Last, but by no means least, I wish to thank my family - Gordon, Greg, and Cami, and my parents Drs. Harry and Clover Jarrett - who provided a constant source of strength; for understanding how much this book means to me; for caring for me during countless hours of writing and research; and for loving me through it all.

Table of Contents

Preface		x
Introduction		xi
1	Personal Leadership Vision	1
	Reflective Practice	4
2	Get to Know Your Students as Individuals	10
	Reflective Practice	14
3	My First Few Days as a Teacher	17
	Reflective Practice	22
4	Determine the Learning Strategies of your Students	27
	Reflective Practice	29
5	I am a Change Agent	31
	Reflective Practice	32
6	Strategies to Support Students along the way	39
	Reflective Practice	41
7	Monitor the Progress of Students	47
	Reflective Practice	49
8	Time Management	53
	Reflective Practice	55

9	Allow Students to Think	61
	Reflective Practice	65
10	Multiple Intelligences	74
	Reflective Practice	77

Summative Exercises *(Primary School Students)*	79
Summative Exercises *(High School Students)*	84
References	99
About the Author	100

Preface

THE HANDBOOK FOR STUDENT-TEACHERS: RAISING LEADERS IN THE CLASSROOM comes at an important moment when there is a strong need to transform nations through education. It will help new teachers as they seek to be effective in serving the needs of students in this globalized era.

This Handbook guides the individual teacher to become a Master Teacher which is a major investment towards their future in the classroom. Most importantly, the immediate tasks of student-teacher are to take control of, and manage their learning with the focal point being on developing leaders in the classroom. The Handbook is designed to become a resource to be utilized when questions arise in classrooms of today. It creatively outlines how cultivating leadership in the classroom can be enhanced. This resource will be highly beneficial when designing and revising student leadership programs in primary and high schools.

To gain full value from this book, it is recommended that teachers complete the activities from each chapter. As you work through the book, you will find that the topics are interrelated.

As new teachers delve into the important ideas on the following pages, I am confident, that even though leadership development is a challenge for the future, success will come when we exhibit that we are role models in the classroom. This will bridge the gap in leadership development and will result in new horizons being created for years to come.

Introduction

The opportunity to work directly with students in the new classroom carries many responsibilities for the new teacher. These responsibilities are enumerated below:

- Employing Principles that engage all learners
- Refining their Personal Leadership Vision
- Learning Curricula expectations
- Applying knowledge learned from Student-Teacher Programs

The first few weeks of school will not create a 'polished' teacher, but rather provide opportunities for growth. Each new teacher should approach teaching with an honest and sincere desire to be a Master Teacher and endeavour to learn about the following topics:

- Student
- Classroom
- School
- School Environment

CHECKLIST FOR THE STUDENT-TEACHER

This Checklist is designed to offer suggestions to new teachers to get them started during the first few weeks of school. It is recommended that the forms included in the Handbook be utilized when developing leaders in the classroom.

CHECKLIST FOR STUDENT-TEACHERS

THE STUDENT				
	Yes	No	Not Required	Comments
Do you have relevant information about each student?				
Do you listen to student conversations?				
Do you have a good rapport with students?				
Is there positive interaction among students?				
Do you record the interests of students?				
Are techniques used to discover the Learning Styles of students?				

THE CLASSROOM				
	Yes	No	Not Required	Comments
Do you know the procedures for new teachers to secure needed supplies?				

THE CLASSROOM

	Yes	No	Not Required	Comments
Do you get the attention of students at the start of the lesson?				
Do questions stimulate appropriate responses from students?				
Are assignments challenging for students?				
Are you experiencing problems with Classroom Management?				
Do you anticipate behavioural problems?				

THE SCHOOL

	Yes	No	Not Required	Comments
Do you know what the organizational structure of the school looks like?				
Are teaching resources (textbooks, supplies, and aids) available?				
Are you informed of the procedures for ordering supplies?				

THE SCHOOL

	Yes	No	Not Required	Comments
Are Special Services available (health, administration, physical education, speech and hearing, custodial)?				
Are teachers involved in the formulation of school policies/rules?				
Does the school serve the needs of the community?				
Do parent activities exist at the school?				
Is there a general positive attitude of students toward school?				

THE SCHOOL ENVIRONMENT

	Yes	No	Not Required	Comments
Do you know the geographical area served by the school?				
Are there special programs available in the school system?				

THE SCHOOL ENVIRONMENT

	Yes	No	Not Required	Comments
Does the school and the community collaborate on projects?				

Chapter 1~

PERSONAL LEADERSHIP VISION

As new teachers, we are exposed to new ideas. It is important that we know where these ideas fit in the classroom, and then focus on how to become skilled at utilizing them. Envisioning the classroom you want is the first step in the journey to the vision becoming a reality. New teachers articulate their vision to the students and engage them in shared classroom discussions on what is important to the members of the class, which will result in collective beliefs, common direction, and the energy generated to pursue it. It all begins with a Personal Leadership Vision.

Personal Leadership Vision gives meaning and purpose to the work required. New teachers are expected to be knowledgeable, committed to, and skilled in the following areas:

- working with all students in a manner which is equitable, caring, and effective
- embracing diversity in relation to gender, ethnicity, race, and special needs of each learner
- developing and applying knowledge of the curriculum and instruction, and
- developing a personal teaching philosophy

It is paramount that new teachers engage their students in a vision-building process. Students will, in turn, own, commit, and become energized toward making this vision a reality. A shared vision takes the following points into consideration:

- Quality Teaching and Learning
- Characteristics of students and families
- Desired goals (cognitive, affective, social, and physical)
- Hopes and aspirations
- Dreams for the future of students
- High expectations

If the vision is truly shared, it will be evident in the climate (how the students' feel) and culture (setting of the rules governing behaviour) of the classroom.

Having a Personal Leadership Vision helps new teachers to 'stop and think' of what their expectations are, and how to help students to make good choices. A teacher may choose to use conflict resolution skills to deal with situations where students are involved in conflicts in the classroom.

Sometimes new teachers experience a conflict between their own values, beliefs, and vision and those existing in the class. This conflict is sometimes accepted by the way experienced teachers pass it off as "this is the way things are done around here." The new teacher will then realize that the culture of the classroom and/or school is not in alignment with their expectations.

Let us examine the real benefits of the shared vision of a master teacher.

The Personal Leadership Vision of the master teacher is that feeling that drives, compels, and fills him/her with determination, even in the most overwhelming and stressful circumstances. It is that deeper sense of purpose that fills every moment with meaning and worth. It is the desire of the master teacher to provide learners with engaging hands-on learning opportunities that will enable every area of their development.

The classroom is the place where students encounter unconditional love and care, experience the joy of learning, and discover new things about themselves and their world. It is this vision that enables the master teacher to refocus mentally and continue to do what is best to create a culture of care for students.

Sharing the vision with students is one way to connect with the 'classroom family.' When students know that we set goals for ourselves, they will be encouraged to set their own. When the master teacher has a vision in mind, they will work more effectively for students, no matter the circumstances. Teachers should display their shared vision somewhere in the classroom to remind students why they are there, and to keep them moving forward in challenging times.

REFLECTIVE PRACTICE

SELF REFLECTION: The Way I See Myself and How Others May See Me

THE WAY I SEE MYSELF

Complete the Table and answer the questions below:

QUALITIES, I AM...	ALWAYS	SOMETIMES	NEVER
CONFIDENT			
PUNCTUAL			
HONEST			
ASSERTIVE			
OBSERVANT			
CARING			
CHARISMATIC			
HARDWORKING			
STUBBORN			
KIND			
LOYAL			
CREATIVE			
SOCIABLE			
COMPASSIONATE			
SELFISH			
POSITIVE			
HUMOUROUS			
FRIENDLY			
WITHDRAWN			
COMPULSIVE			
INTELLIGENT			
AMBITIOUS			

PERSONAL LEADERSHIP VISION

State five characteristics that you ranked '**Never**' Like Me

_____
_____
_____
_____
_____

State five characteristics that you ranked '**Always**' Like Me

_____
_____
_____
_____
_____

What two characteristics do I most admire?

_____
_____
_____
_____
_____

HOW OTHERS MAY SEE ME

Complete the Table and answer the questions below:

QUALITIES	FAMILY	PEERS	TEACHERS/ INSTRUCTORS
CONFIDENT			
PUNCTUAL			
HONEST			
ASSERTIVE			
OBSERVANT			
CARING			
CHARISMATIC			
HARDWORKING			
STUBBORN			
KIND			
LOYAL			
CREATIVE			
SOCIABLE			
COMPASSIONATE			
SELFISH			
POSITIVE			
HUMOUROUS			
FRIENDLY			
WITHDRAWN			
COMPULSIVE			
AMBITIOUS			
INTELLIGENCE			

How can I use these characteristics to develop and enhance my life?

What characteristics do I need to improve on?

Name:_____ Date:_____

PERSONAL STRENGTHS & AREAS OF NEED

Using the chart below, list a **MINIMUM** of **Five** Personal Strengths. Also, list a **MINIMUM** of **Five** Personal Areas of Need. Give an example of each strength and need.

Personal Strengths	Areas of Need
1.	1.
2.	2.
3.	3.
4.	4.

PERSONAL LEADERSHIP VISION

Personal Strengths	Areas of Need
5.	5.
6.	6.
7.	7.

Chapter 2~

GET TO KNOW YOUR STUDENTS AS INDIVIDUALS

It is beneficial when teachers display a strong interest in the learning process and have faith in the abilities of their students. Students treasure the personal interest shown by the teacher and in return, they will be loyal and respectful. When this sense of loyalty is displayed, teaching and learning will have new meaning to both the teacher and student, because the environment is created for instruction to be tailored to the learning style and background of the student.

It is important that new teachers understand their students' tastes and peculiar behavioural habits. This understanding can be achieved by building a positive relationship with their students, which helps to minimize the potential of any behavioural problems that can arise in the classroom. The more students know and respect teachers, the more they will behave for them in the classroom.

Let us examine some of the ways teachers can take time to build positive relationships in the classroom.

GET TO KNOW YOUR STUDENTS AS INDIVIDUALS

New teachers should schedule time in Lesson Plans for greeting students. Finding out how each student is doing each day by talking to them one-on-one is good practice. A quick 'Hello' during the first few minutes of a class is an opportunity for the teacher to gauge the student's emotional state and to see whether they are having a good, bad, or not so good a day. If the student looks as though something is going on in his/her life, take the time to stop, and ask, "How are you, today"? "Is there anything you want to talk about"? "Let's talk when I get everyone started on the class assignment". This gesture that shows the student that you care and willing to take time out of your day to talk, is the start of building that relationship. Keep in mind that some students may not want to talk, but others will.

It is not uncommon for a new teacher to come across a student who is very disruptive, constantly annoying, and who goes out of his/her way to make the classroom experience uncomfortable. This situation can be dealt with by using a culture of care, which is constantly showing the student that you care. Never give up on any student. New teachers move one step in the right direction when they get to know each student as a human being, not just as a student. Often, new teachers find themselves quite surprised by the level of intense focus experienced by students while engaged in meaningful learning experiences, and the resulting decline in behavioral problems in the classroom. Over time, talking, listening, and caring earn the respect of students.

It is possible for new teachers to miss individuals in the classroom, if they continue to observe students as a group.

Let us examine the following scenario, which highlights that knowledge of individual students affects possible decisions.

"While working with Sasha at the back of the classroom, Hannah comes to the teacher and says "Pete reached out and hit Tristan." What would be your response?"

Interacting with the class as a group............

The teacher would be inclined to think that Pete deliberately hit Tristan for no apparent reason, and send him to the Office immediately. Pete could feel unjustly punished and start having feelings of resentment toward the teacher. Tristan might celebrate that he tricked the teacher by 'pulling the wool over his/her eyes'. Yay!! Woo Hoo!! Great!!

Interacting with individual students................

Knowing the personality of both Tristan and Pete, the teacher would consider discussing it with them and come to a decision regarding possible consequences. Pete might get a consequence for the mere fact that he hit Tristan, rather than informing the teacher, but not punished as severely as he might have been. Tristan gets a consequence for taunting Pete and understands that this behaviour will be watched, and will not be tolerated in the classroom.

Can you see how knowledge of the individual students can affect possible decisions?

Teachers, unconsciously, bring their physical appearance and culture into the classroom, similar to what students do. The way you look, speak, and act, will have an effect on the interactions in the classroom. It is important to observe the possible reactions among students to your race, gender, age, ethnicity, physical attributes, and abilities.

Know your students well and in the end, word will get around, "Hey, hope you get Mr. Baker next year. He's tough but he's cool"! or "Miss Jacobs is strict but she's a great teacher".

A teacher will be remembered as someone who took the time to treat each student as an individual and as a person, and is loved for it.

REFLECTIVE PRACTICE

GETTING TO KNOW YOU

Write a message to your teacher describing yourself, family, and interests. Please include the following:

a. Music, sports, art, etc.
b. Learning style(s), eg. "I learn best when..."
c. Competition(s) you have participated in
d. Any unique skills or talent, the number of languages you speak
e. Subjects you excel in and those you need assistance with
f. How you plan to be more successful this school year

Add any other information that may be beneficial to your learning needs.

_____
_____
_____
_____
_____
_____
_____
_____
_____
_____
_____
_____
_____
_____
_____
_____

GET TO KNOW YOUR STUDENTS AS INDIVIDUALS

RAISING LEADERS IN THE CLASSROOM

Chapter 3~

MY FIRST FEW DAYS AS A TEACHER

Teachers are expected to listen to their students; teach their class; prepare class material; design formative assessments; plan meaningful units; practise interpreting standards; supervise lunchroom/playground during recess time; attend parent meetings; complete relevant forms; and a host of other responsibilities.

Teachers, who like young people and value their opinions, should practise active listening in the classroom. Good listening skills allow the teacher to make sense of, and understand what their students are saying, resulting in improved teacher preparation. For listening to take place in the learning environment, the teacher should be persistent, patient, and attentive. Teachers need to encourage students to speak their minds in structured and unstructured settings, in order to meet their learning needs more effectively.

Listen to:

1. YOUR STUDENTS

Listening to your students is just as important as speaking with them. By asking students their thoughts, they will feel that you hear their concerns and questions. They will tell you and you will learn from it. Listen, nod, and respond appropriately, when students speak.

Avoid assuming you know what the students are going to say. Answer only when the student has completely finished speaking. Use your body language to show you are listening to the student by doing the following:

- Restating what the student said
- Pausing before responding which will give yourself time to think about what the student said
- Asking the student, if necessary, to come to a conclusion and then paraphrasing what was said
- Asking yourself what key point the student is making.

Listening to students, offers the teacher an opportunity to reflect on their instruction, which can result in students taking ownership of their learning. It can also lead to a higher level of student motivation.

2. THE DISCUSSIONS OF STUDENTS

Listening tends to be a neglected literacy skill in the classroom. It can take place informally by walking around in hallways, peering into different classrooms, and observing students being inattentive, daydreaming, and whispering to one another.

What would the students say if they were asked about the kinds of teaching they are exposed to every day?

Before engaging in a conversation with students, the teacher can create a climate for students to voice their feelings by telling them a little about themselves, and by asking the student a little about him/herself, in a relaxed manner.

Each student has their own experiences and the teacher can learn a lot by engaging them in meaningful discussions by asking the following questions:

- Tell me about your class?
- Do you enjoy learning?
- What are you learning in your class right now?

Teachers can make other positive changes in the classroom and the whole school environment by getting more specific. Students can be asked carefully and respectfully, the following questions:

- What is it that is working for you or what is not?
- What could help you learn better?

3. THE QUESTIONS OF STUDENTS

Sometimes it is clear what your student is asking and you can provide a response or suggest people who can offer help. It is not always clear what is being asked and we might find that more information is necessary. Always check your understanding of their question.

Should students show an interest in having a discussion with you, be clear and precise about your time availability. For example, "I can give you five minutes.............." rather than "I only have 5 minutes..........."

Sensitive matters may require some documentation, and seeking permission to record it, can be helpful. To offer some assurance, the student can be invited to view the notes before they leave.

4. WHAT STUDENTS ARE STRUGGLING WITH

Students will not work if they do not know how, even if it is engaging. They have to be motivated and organized to do it. Teachers can meet as a team, discuss the strengths of the students, and ask students to indicate the supports needed to complete their assignment. Teachers must seek from the student or create an individual plan with one or two specific strategies to assist them with their concerns. Both teacher and student should document this together, so future reference is available.

5. WHERE STUDENTS ARE MAKING ERRORS

Teachers should keep the correction experience positive for the learner. In the learning environment, identify the errors your students are making; remember to listen for the proper use of language and new vocabulary; and allow enough time to highlight these to the group.

Teachers should take into consideration that the constant correction of a student can be really de-motivating. Depending on the activity, teachers can sometimes invite ideas on how students would like to be corrected.

Let us examine the Traffic Light Correction Circle as a Correction Activity (Budden, 2010).

Students are given a strip of cards with three circles and an arrow.

Each colour has the following meaning:

RED - Don't correct me at all (I'm tired or had a rough day)

YELLOW - Correct me with things that are really important or with things I ought to know

GREEN - Correct me as much as possible, please

Students use the arrow to indicate whether or not they want correction.

Another Correction Activity that the new teacher can use in the classroom is the Mistake/Correction Table (Budden, 2010).

MISTAKES	CORRECTIONS	NOTES
I checked the whether this morning	I checked the weather this morning	Revise homonyms

This correction strategy can be used to help students avoid repeating the same mistakes. New mistakes are usually an indication that the students are exploring new uses of the language and new vocabulary.

Too often, we focus on the script and lesson plan and simply want to execute it. It can become very confusing, when the flow of our lesson is interrupted by students.

REFLECTIVE PRACTICE

CASE STUDY

Miss James looked around the classroom and found that Samantha had the answer to her question, and said, "Aha! You've got it!" She generalized that the whole class got it and carried on with the flow of the lesson.

Should the focus be on what Miss James had planned or the impact she is having on all her students and their learning? Explain.

_____
_____
_____
_____
_____
_____
_____
_____
_____

The focus should be on listening to what the students are saying and observing what students are doing. In order to have a high probability for learning to occur, it is important that effective communication and listening skills are utilized in the classroom learning environment.

The biggest concern of a student, whenever they ask questions is, "What are my peers going to say?" Teachers should convey to the students that it is acceptable not to have all the answers.

REFLECTIVE QUESTIONS

Which of these teacher statements are DOs or DON'Ts?

1. I bet that makes you feel (sad, happy.....................)
2. Can I make sure I got this right............................?
3. Can you tell me about your day.................?
4. That must be terrible..................!
5. I only have five minutes.....................

NEW TEACHER REFLECTION

1. How should you act when a student disrupts the class?

_____
_____
_____
_____
_____
_____
_____

2. How do you think a student feels when you single them out for praise/criticism?

_____
_____
_____
_____
_____
_____
_____

3. Outline two rookie errors that a teacher may commit

4. Identify three problems a teacher may encounter on the first few days of school?

5. State two signals students may show when they are bored?

6. List two motivational strategies the teacher can employ to minimize boredom?

7. List three factors that may cause performance anxiety for students?

8. Identify four strategies that a teacher can adopt to ensure effective classroom management

Chapter 4~

DETERMINE THE LEARNING STRATEGIES OF YOUR STUDENTS

In the classrooms of today, students are expected to find and use information, and are therefore, no longer required to memorize and repeat information. Most importantly, the role of teachers has shifted to helping students to develop their intellectual capabilities and learning strategies, in order for them to acquire knowledge and engage in productive thinking. Teachers create a win-win situation when they expose students to the learning strategies that can best help them to understand the course content. Therefore, it is vital to encourage students to apply, synthesize, and evaluate information that will promote success in the learning environment.

Students will benefit significantly, when they are aware of their learning styles. Students are, often times, considered reluctant learners and unprepared in the learning environment. The real reason may be that they were not actively involved in identifying their learning style which can be attributed to them not knowing how to learn.

LEARNING STYLES

A Learning Style is how we like to learn. The three main Learning Styles are:

Visual Learners

Visual Learners tend to like when they receive information by seeing it. They focus a lot on details and generally are not very talkative. Use of maps, graphs, and pictures are very beneficial to them.

Auditory Learners

Auditory Learners tend to learn best when they receive ideas and information by hearing them. Memorizing the lyrics of a song is what they may excel at, yet struggle with reading and writing. Providing them with opportunities to do oral presentations and discussion-based classes can enhance their learning.

Kinesthetic-Tactile Learners

Kinesthetic-Tactile Learners prefer to learn via movement and touch. They are very active and tend not to sit for long periods. Note-taking activities should be encouraged, while these learners get involved, explore, and experience their environment.

Most people have a dominant Learning Style. Educators need to be sensitive while they are providing the opportunity for all students to succeed by creating more inclusive classrooms. It may be challenging for a student to participate in class activities when they are from a culture that teaches students to listen quietly in the classroom.

REFLECTIVE PRACTICE

Let us give some thought to enhancing student learning.

Describe two ways that students can benefit from collaborating with their peers in small or large groups?

How will students learn from taking extensive notes?

How can students be taught to engage in discussions or debates?

How would students benefit from being taught how to ask questions?

Chapter 5~

I AM A CHANGE AGENT

New teachers need to enter the classroom on the first few days of school with a 'change orientation' approach, which involves a strong commitment to new ideas and the will and tenacity to deal with the unknown. It is important to feel empowered to make deliberate and thoughtful changes in the classroom. New teachers should allow their curiosity and sense of wonder to be stimulated.

Research shows that teachers in their third year implement learning strategies much less often than they had done in the first two years. Therefore, new teachers should continue to strive to maintain the level of passion, commitment, and vision, well into their teaching careers. This will help bridge the gap because, in reality, if some students had the choice they would not come to school and do what we assign them anyway. These students only attend school because society has decided it is important.

REFLECTIVE PRACTICE

Name the teachers that have had the greatest impact on your life?

How did they help to change you?

I AM A CHANGE AGENT

_____
_____
_____
_____
_____

It takes a lot of energy to be a change agent. There will be days as a new teacher, that you will feel that everyone around you is withholding information or unwilling to offer support. It is that burning passion that the teacher experiences that allows them to rise every day and go to work. The high energy exhibited by the new teacher risks them being misunderstood and unappreciated by their colleagues, administration, and parents. Those who have concerns for the new teacher are thinking of burn-out and frustration that they will experience. The new teacher persists because it is known that the real rewards of educational excellence are in the future.

Teachers have the ability to achieve great things, both inside and outside the classroom. It is imperative that new teachers are very aware and ready for action. Teachers are closest to the problem of student learning and should be the agents of change; they help the school administration to know what resources are necessary to enhance the school environment, and then the information can be utilized to improve student learning. Teachers are change agents when they make their contributions to improving the school by reaching beyond the classroom into the community.

Some new teachers are driven to improve teaching practices and/or student achievement in their schools. When teachers are comfortable with both students and colleagues, it allows for effective participation in the change process between individual classrooms and the school as a whole. Teachers, who possess the skill to improve teaching practices, tend to spot trends in the classroom and the school environment and articulate them to their peers. This action exemplifies their commitment to the reform of current school practices.

It is vital that new teachers possess an open mind about their school and have a heightened sense of being, in order to effect interactions with their colleagues. To be a change agent, new teachers need to have a feeling of personal responsibility to do so. Working with peers can be a creative experience because individuals get a chance to think 'outside the box,' are highly motivated, and comfortable as a team in making decisions (Lukacs, 2014).

REFLECTIVE PRACTICE

CASE STUDY

Devin, while on duty on the playground, witnessed a short display of bullying. He complained about this bullying incident in the Staff Meeting held the following week. He did not follow-up on the incident with the Guidance Counsellors, as was suggested.

Jenn was disturbed by the same aggressive incident that Devin witnessed, and watched as the student bystanders gloried in the presence of their peers. She collaborated with a team of teachers and established an anti-bullying program that included a classroom discussion about bullying and rehearsing with students what they might say when they see bullying taking place.

Compare and contrast the change orientation approach adopted by Devin and Jenn.

Describe five ways in which new teachers can effectively improve a school environment.

Compare and contrast the role of teachers and administrators, as agents of change, within the school environment

New teachers should understand the various processes within the school and have a strong professional relationship with colleagues and administration. Team teaching, with subject-alike and grade-alike teachers in their school, is a great way to reflect, revise, and improve delivery. New teachers can benefit a lot from team teaching; they are put on teams with other teachers - same grade-level, same subject-area, interdisciplinary team (English, History, Math, Science). Teachers may sometimes need to specialize more, as some already do, and share responsibility for students in a way that says, "You teach my combined Math and Science class and I'll teach your Language Arts and Social Studies class".

Let us examine the strategies that can be implemented when new Curriculum gets added during the school year.

Take one of three lessons in the unit and then rotate through the groups of students. Instead of preparing for three lessons, teachers would only do one class, which is a definite time saver. Teachers are able to meet lesson learning criteria when they coordinate lessons with other teachers. Another effective way to improve student learning across grade levels is to exchange homogeneous grouping of students.

Let us examine the ways that team teaching can assist in the process to becoming master teachers. Teachers can take advantage of team teaching in the following ways:

- discuss the pedagogical content
- share beliefs about the curriculum being taught
- discuss textbooks, equipment, and tools being used
- identify the abilities of students in the class
- propose ideas to each other
- exchange ideas dealing with classroom management

- freely express themselves
- get feedback on questions/concerns

It is important that teachers take the time individually and in groups to create the quality instruction needed for our students. Teachers need planning time with grade-alike and subject-alike teachers who can help them understand the sequence and scope of each subject area. When teachers become involved in Interactive Professionalism it helps them to design formative assessments; plan challenging units; and practise and interpret standards.

Planning time allows teachers to be more effective in the following ways:

- establish a quiet time and reflect
- provide more time for preparing lessons and activities (photocopying, research topics, grade and record answers)
- provide time for self-renewal
- contact parents

Chapter 6~

STRATEGIES TO SUPPORT STUDENTS ALONG THE WAY

There are days when students will not be enthusiastic about a lesson; other days when they will question the reason for doing an activity, project, assignment, or test; and days when an assessment was scheduled and they are not getting it. Regardless of the value of a topic or activity, sometimes Lesson Plans that are exciting do not seem to have the same effect when presented to the class. What teachers think will translate into great lessons, if the students do not recognize its value, they may not be motivated to expend effort.

Let us examine the following teaching strategies:

- Communicate Learning Goals: New teachers should start preparing for their students with learning goals by thinking of the topics, concepts, skills, and areas of learning connected to the lesson. By preparing a number of lesson plans, the teacher would have developed the expertise in the process. Teachers should aim to maximize the number of teaching goals per lesson thereby increasing the probability of conveying the relevant concepts.

Teachers know the most important concepts that should be mastered by students. It is important that learning goals are stated clearly for each lesson, so that when required, students can explain the concepts that were presented. These goals outline the skills, knowledge, and perspectives of the lesson and should be posted in the classroom for students to see. The display reminds students about how the activities relate to the learning goal. It is more meaningful to students when the teacher makes reference to the scale or rubric throughout the lesson, and students will be able to articulate the meaning of the levels of performance. Learning goals provide a road map that guides students through the learning process. When goals are outlined, there is direction for both student and teacher. Communicating these goals, aid the teacher in selecting appropriate and graded assessments, which is a value-added element in the teaching and learning process.

- Provide a Degree of Choice: Teachers should allow students the freedom of choosing topics for projects, which will serve to connect the course content to their outside interests and passion. In order to motivate students, it is sometimes necessary to restrict topic options so that students do not get overwhelmed with too many choices. Academic performance can be governed by learning contracts that provide descriptions of the curriculum expectations for both teacher and student. It allows students to choose and be guided by relevant factors, such as, selecting group partners, choosing alternate assignments, and determining their due dates and assignments. These options can help students to feel some sense of autonomy and take ownership and responsibility for their educational development and success.

REFLECTIVE PRACTICE

Outline **three** ways that Learning Contracts may be utilized in the classroom?

_____
_____
_____
_____
_____
_____
_____
_____
_____
_____
_____
_____

- Passion and Discovery: Teachers can have a powerful and contagious effect on students, if they show their own enthusiasm about the course content. When excitement is felt in the classroom, it will raise the level of curiosity of the student, which leads to more discoveries in the content.
- Stimulate Personal Interests: Lessons are enhanced when teachers connect course material to personal interests. Teachers who create learning activities based on topics that are relevant to the lives of their students, foster a sense of intrinsic motivation. Teachers can be creative and connect topics with culture, outside interests, and social lives of students by introducing current news events,

IPads, Cell phones, Social Media, and YouTube videos in the lesson.

In the classroom, students sometimes react in different ways to subjects, topics, and tasks.

Let us review what happened in a Grade 4 Elementary Geography Class relating to a lesson in Weather Reporting.

Both John and Joe are taking Science in Elementary School and learning how to report the weather. John finds the topic boring, spends limited time practising, and often has incomplete assignments. Joe, on the other hand, enjoys checking daily temperatures and reporting to the class, and even expands his knowledge by comparing the temperatures with other countries.

Students tend to devote more attention if they are interested in the topic, than when their learning is based on effort. Sometimes students are inclined to have interest in nonacademic subjects (music, sports, celebrities), which can be conflicting in the classroom and to keep them aroused, the teacher can include trivia questions at appropriate points in the lesson. This would be an opportunity for teachers to reward students with strong general knowledge skills. Teachers can also provide colourful illustrations, pictures, or YouTube Videos as a stimulating exercise. Another strategy is to add interesting pieces of information to a written or verbal explanation. Teachers can, occasionally, find ways to include surprises in their comments, while doing activities. Teachers can also provide opportunities for students to respond to new material by having them talk about it together in small groups or class discussions, thereby giving them the chance to make their own personal connections. However, teachers should avoid distracting students with inappropriate material, which can create misunderstanding and lead them away from the focus of the lesson. Often times, the struggling students are the ones distracted.

REFLECTIVE PRACTICE

Prepare a lesson that can be used to connect course material in any chosen subject area, to the personal interests of students.

STRATEGIES TO SUPPORT STUDENTS

Suggested Classroom Phrases!

"Just wait to see how exciting the next assignment is!"

"It's amazing how creative you are! I think this is cool!"

"I like to see how you're thinking, because I notice some of you are asking about X. We're finally going to discover X."

Chapter 7~

MONITORING THE PROGRESS OF STUDENTS

Taking the time to provide constant feedback on the work of students, helps the teacher to assess whether the student understands what is expected of them. Students who are not meeting curriculum expectations should be provided with the necessary assistance to develop their competence and skills. It is important that teachers monitor the progress of their students in order to promote success in the classroom.

The following benefits can be derived by the teacher from daily monitoring:

- Provides an overview of how each student feels in the class.
- Explains the concepts that students are misunderstanding.
- Determines if they need extra time for submitting work.
- Ascertains the various ways the students can be given the best help.

At the Elementary School level, teachers can provide support to students by walking around the classroom every day, signing Planners. The purpose of this writing in the Planners is a means of communication between the school and the parent/guardian regarding any change in behaviour and academic performance.

The daily process of monitoring students includes the following:
- observing students while on task.
- posing questions which asks students to describe their tasks and how the tasks make them feel.
- providing feedback to students while talking with them.
- writing notes, comments, or suggestions which serves as reference points for discussions.

Students should receive feedback promptly, and it is crucial that teachers keep graded work updated. Teachers are expecting students to complete and submit assignments and tests in the agreed time; similarly, students are expected to have their tests, projects, assignments returned in a timely manner. This expectation will result in students being more up-to-date with their progress.

Testing and evaluation should be one of the focal points in the learning process. Teachers use this opportunity to check for understanding and misunderstanding at the end of lessons or units. While integrating with students, teachers should take the opportunity to focus on their teaching style; evaluate their own performance; and adjust their lesson presentation to suit the different learning styles present in the classroom.

MONITORING THE PROGRESS OF STUDENTS

REFLECTIVE PRACTICE

Using the Student Tracking Sheets (A & B) below, communicate a 5-day continuous progress, to a student and his/her guardian/caregiver.

Student Tracking Sheet (A)

Date: _____ Name: _____

Time	Day 1	Day 2	Day 3	Day 4	Day 5
8 – 9am					
9 – 10am					
10 –11am					
11 –12pm					

RAISING LEADERS IN THE CLASSROOM

Time	Day 1	Day 2	Day 3	Day 4	Day 5
12 – 1pm					
1 – 2pm					
2 – 3pm					
3 – 4pm					
4 - 5pm					
5 – 6pm					

MONITORING THE PROGRESS OF STUDENTS

Student Tracking Sheet (B)

Date: _____ Name: _____

Date	Activity	Comments

Date	Activity	Comments

Chapter 8~

TIME MANAGEMENT

Time Management plays a big part in almost every aspect of what we do daily in the classroom. There is usually less time than what we envision, once teaching starts every day. A teacher rarely accomplishes everything that he/she ideally would like to get done. On a daily basis, teachers are expected to balance the long-term goals of the classroom, the immediate needs of students, and the large volume of paperwork.

Let us consider the number one problem for most teachers, which is that of Paperwork.

Paperwork includes tests, reports, attendance forms, graphs, letters, memos, emails, announcements, materials, late slips, and requests. Teachers should develop good organizational skills to deal with the vast quantity of paperwork they encounter. This allows them to manage their daily routines more effectively, thereby providing time for feedback with the students. It is important that teachers become proficient at multitasking, so that they can manage and direct activities in the classroom environment simultaneously.

Using time efficiently is an essential skill. Teachers should make a list of what needs to be done on Post-it Notes or School Diaries/Planners and schedule their time in order to complete various tasks in a single day.

Although the tasks below do not constitute an extensive list, the following are some of the responsibilities of a teacher:

- Administrative tasks: responding to emails, checking planners, parent contacts, emergencies
- Lesson Planning
- Marking
- Worksheet/Resources Preparation
- Classroom Displays

Teachers should allow themselves time for administrative issues, explaining and reviewing of test procedures and assignments, addressing questions from the lesson, setting up technology, and rearranging the classroom. Maximum results can be gained when teachers estimate the time needed for each task and monitor each activity throughout the day. In order for the lessons to run smoothly, it is important for teachers to work through exercises before the lesson, which will allow them to identify potential challenging areas.

Let us examine the ways that new teachers can help to make their lessons run smoothly.

- Explain what the class will be doing next day. Students tend to get in a positive mood and they will look forward for tomorrow. Upbeat expectations for both student and teacher can create that mood that has a positive effect on learning in the classroom.
- Assign homework for more practice time on a learning concept. Students can be allowed to trade homework and class assignments with their peers, and check their

work from teacher-guided solutions. This activity frees up some time for the new teacher.
- Make use of time-controlled activities, such as, group work, in-class writing, and role playing.
- Display an outline for the day, in addition to the overall goal for the day, in an appropriate place in the classroom.

REFLECTIVE PRACTICE

Record on the Time Tracking Sheets (C & D) below, details of how one day out of the past week, was spent.

Time Tracking Sheet (C)

Date: _____ Name: _____

Time	Activity	Do you feel you spent your time well? Explain
5:00 – 6:00am		
6:00 – 7:00am		
7:00 – 8:00am		
8:00 – 9:00am		
9:00 – 10:00am		
10:00 – 11:00am		
11:00 – 12:00pm		
12:00 – 1:00pm		
1:00 – 2:00pm		
2:00 – 3:00pm		

TIME MANAGEMENT

Time	Activity	Do you feel you spent your time well? Explain
3:00 – 4:00pm		
4:00 -5:00pm		
5:00 – 6:00pm		
6:00 – 7:00pm		
7:00 – 8:00pm		
8:00 – 9:00pm		
9:00 - 10:00pm		
10:00 – 11:00pm		
11:00 – 12:00am		

Time Tracking Sheet (D)

Date: _____ Name: _____

Date	Activity	Comments

TIME MANAGEMENT

Date	Activity	Comments

Using specific examples, state whether you think your day was spent wisely?

_____
_____
_____
_____
_____
_____
_____
_____
_____
_____
_____
_____
_____

Were there tasks/activities that were not completed in that day? If so, state the reasons.

_____
_____
_____
_____
_____
_____
_____
_____
_____
_____
_____

Chapter 9~

ALLOW STUDENTS TO THINK

Students should be encouraged to think in a divergent manner, and not merely to reproduce content, procedures and solutions without thought. New teachers should be equipped with skills to help a diverse range of students to understand and transform content.

The following strategies can be used to ensure that students are decision-makers in their learning environment:

- <u>Differentiated Instruction</u>

    Teachers should always be seeking ways to reach out to their students by providing them with experiences and tasks to improve their learning. Students have different learning styles; different ways to express themselves; and different ways to process information. Therefore, it is important for teachers to use theory, research, and hands-on activities to maximize the learning experiences of each student in the classroom.

- <u>Cooperative Learning</u>

    Cooperative Learning is an instructional strategy which develops the academic and social skills in learners. Students are placed in small groups and work together on structured activities. Accountability is placed on the individual student and also, on the group as a whole, for the work done.

- <u>Questioning</u>

    Teachers should teach Questioning skills to help students to have the tools to comprehend and explore the concepts being presented. Questioning skills are taught when teachers model these skills in the classroom with the questions they ask their students. Use open-ended questions and avoid questions that solicit Yes/No answers. Pose questions that encourage answers that involve critical thinking.

- <u>Scaffolding</u>

    In Scaffolding instruction, the teacher facilitates the learning of new concepts in a lesson by incorporating tasks or activities that are broken down into achievable sections. Graphics, cue cards, and charts can be used as learning supports which help to minimize confusion, stress, and anxiety. Scaffolding instruction promotes open-ended problem-solving and independence. It is recommended that students are given structured talking time on a regular basis. Think-Pair-Share is one of the Scaffolding Techniques that teachers will find very helpful. The teacher can utilize Think-Pair-Share in lessons when they want to encourage cooperative discussion and limit off-task thinking and off-task behaviour.

Let us examine one of the ways that Think-Pair-Share can be incorporated into a lesson.

The teacher can create a research process or source, for students to use the Think-Pair-Share activity. Students will then be asked to evaluate the topic independently, jot down words, phrases, or ideas, and to complete a graphic organizer. Students will be required to work in small groups to discuss the topic and share their thoughts with their group members. Think-Pair-Share is an activity that is used by teachers to support instruction, particularly when they want their students to explore topics.

- Inquiry-Based Learning

    Students are active learners in the Inquiry-based Learning environment and encouraged to ask questions and form their own theories. Both the teacher and the student inquire together, generating theories, and testing ideas. This makes it a community of learners in the classroom, rather than the traditional approach whereby the teacher would transmit answers to the student. The benefits of Inquiry-based Learning are tremendous, as it can guide learning and creative thinking that can last a lifetime and also, helps students to make connections which are important outcomes in the classroom.

Students need good thinking skills for life beyond the classroom which can be achieved if teaching is directed far beyond the goals of testing. Teachers often engage in the following decisions for students:

- Which seats to assign to students
- What order to complete tasks
- What types of books to read
- How many words to write for a project or assignment
- How much to eat at lunchtime
- What students learn
- How students learn

The classroom should be a perfect place for students to learn how to think and make decisions. Elementary students should be encouraged to develop tools and strategies to problem-solve and meet their own needs. The teacher should provide opportunities for students to involve themselves in goal setting; engage in class meetings; analyze class and school issues and concerns; and learn how to volunteer within the community. When a student is trained in problem-solving and decision making, it will lay the foundation for them to become lifelong learners.

REFLECTIVE PRACTICE

To what extent should students be allowed to think for themselves?

___
___
___
___
___
___
___
___
___
___
___
___
___

It is important that teachers include lifetime questions posed by students into the required curriculum, which is an effective way in teaching students that the curriculum is authentic and that teachers are concerned about their lives. If students have a legitimate voice in the curriculum, it will help them solve societal problems, interact with peers and community, and explore the world of their future. Increased student motivation, better relationships between and among students, and increased student achievement, are all results of an integrated curriculum.

REFLECTIVE PRACTICE

State two benefits to be derived from planning lessons that prepare students for society and their future

_____
_____
_____
_____
_____
_____
_____
_____
_____
_____
_____
_____
_____
_____

What is the impact of television, technology, video games, internet, unsafe neighborhood, lack of parental involvement and support, on student achievement?

_____
_____
_____
_____
_____
_____
_____
_____
_____

Assess the effectiveness of the Integrated Curriculum on the accomplishments of students?

Describe two strategies that the teacher can use to encourage students to take ownership of their learning

Generate three classroom rules and consequences.

Cultural Diversity

Teachers can respond to cultural diversity in many ways; they can infuse art and music from different cultures. Students can expand their knowledge about different cultures by reading relevant literature, visiting museums, participating in plays, and conducting research projects.

Special Needs

Classrooms should be designed in a way that respects children with special needs. For students to hear and see clearer, they should be given seating positions in the front of the classroom. It is most often beneficial to have students with visual and hearing impairments sit in groups beside buddies who can provide that extra help. It is imperative that teachers make modifications to their teaching strategies. Students with Special Needs should also be given opportunities to think on their own by allowing them to work on projects in a group that they have selected.

Conflict Resolution

A conflict is a serious disagreement; dispute; friction; fight; argument; or feeling of opposition. It is normal and healthy for new teachers to experience their share of conflict in the classroom.

Consider the classroom environment for a moment.

What are some of the key sources of conflict that will develop in the classroom?

When do they tend to occur?

How should the teacher respond to these conflicts when they arise?

In reflecting upon your responses to these questions, the approach of a new teacher should be to anticipate conflicts, which is useful in transforming these situations into opportunities for growth and learning.

Practising good communication skills will help the parties involved in a conflict to reflect on the following suggestions:
- Focus on the other person's point of view.
- Inspire the other person to respond with a kind gesture.
- Find a resolution that both sides are comfortable with.

REFLECTIVE PRACTICE

Why are good communication skills important?

_____
_____
_____
_____
_____
_____
_____
_____
_____
_____
_____
_____
_____
_____

State THREE situations where you would use good communication skills to resolve a conflict

_____
_____
_____
_____
_____
_____
_____
_____
_____
_____
_____

Identify THREE ways that an individual can improve their communication skills

What may be the impact of poor communication skills?

ALLOW STUDENTS TO THINK

Chapter 10~

MULTIPLE INTELLIGENCES

We all learn in different ways. There are some things that a student will enjoy, while some things will be disliked. The new teacher should reassure students that no style is better than the other. There will be times when they have to produce work using a type of Intelligence that is not their favourite, but because it is the best way to get the task done.

Multiple Intelligences will guide teachers to teach differently. Howard Gardner defined several types of Intelligences which reinforces that each child in the classroom has a value and contribution to make to the whole group. According to Gardner's theory, we are all able to view the world through linguistic analysis, logical-mathematical reasoning, spatial imagery, musical reflection, body language, interactions with others, and through independent study (Campbell, 1996).

Having information on the most dominant type of Intelligence for each student will help teachers to make informed decisions as to how to address the needs of each student. The teacher will become knowledgeable of how to effectively challenge, motivate, and accommodate students in the classroom.

MULTIPLE INTELLIGENCES

Let us examine the ways in which we can teach students about Multiple Intelligences.

1. Assign tasks to students.

2. Ask students to use different Multiple Intelligences in completing the following tasks:

    - Interpret numeric data
    - Pay attention to a piece of music
    - Solve a logic puzzle
    - Use bodies to represent a concept
    - Work with other students
    - Classify natural items

Multiple Intelligences Guide

	TYPES OF INTELLIGENCE	ATTRIBUTES	CAREERS
1	VERBAL (WORD SMART)	Conversations, Debates, Long emails, Class discussions	Teachers, Lawyers, Politicians, Leaders
2	LOGISTICAL (NUMBER SMART)	Formula building, Problem-solving	Computer Programmers, Actuarial Scientists
3	MUSICAL (RHYTHMIC SMART)	Rhythmic Language, Emotions sensitive	Composers, Conductors, Musicians
4	VISUAL (PICTURE SMART)	Imaginations, Pictures, Creativity	Architects, Sculptors, Pilots, Artists, Building Contractors
5	PHYSICAL (BODY SMART)	Body Building	Athletes, Dancers
6	INTERPERSONAL / SOCIAL (PEOPLE SMART)	Speeches, Empathy, Understanding	Sales People, Negotiators, Motivational Speakers, Coaches
7	INTRAPERSONAL / INTUITIVE (FEELING SMART)	Intuition, Motives, Feelings, Reserved	Psychologists, Guidance Counselors
8	NATURALIST / NATURE (NATURE SMART)	Outdoors, Agriculture, Animals	Farmers, Fishermen, Veterinarians, Biologist, Environmentalists
9	PHILOSOPHICAL / HUMANATARIAN (SPIRIT SMART)	Social Clubs, Community Churches, History, Politics	Politicians, Ministers of Religion, Motivational Speakers, Social Leaders

REFLECTIVE PRACTICE

In the chart on the following page, list **six** occupations/careers that are likely to fall under each type of Intelligence. Use the previous chart as a guide.

Multiple Intelligences Chart

	Nature	Feelings	People	Body	Picture	Spiritual	Music	Number	Word

SUMMATIVE EXERCISES

(Primary School Students)

MY JOURNAL

Date: _____ Name: _____

The leader I admire the most _____

_____
_____
_____
_____
_____
_____
_____
_____
_____
_____
_____
_____
_____
_____
_____
_____
_____
_____
_____
_____
_____
_____
_____
_____
_____
_____

RAISING LEADERS IN THE CLASSROOM

CREATING LEADERS

Date: _____ Name: _____

1. In the Chart below, list **three** great leaders. List **three** of their qualities (for example, honest or brave).

LEADERS	QUALITIES

2. a) Create your ideal Caribbean Leader
   b) Give your leader a name
   c) Write a short description by using some of the qualities from your chart.

OR

3. a) Create a slogan for your ideal Caribbean Leader
   b) Give your leader a name
   c) Make a poster of your leader

SUMMATIVE EXERCISES

(High School Students)

DISCOVERING CARIBBEAN GREATS

Date: _____

Name of Teacher: _____
Name of Student: _____

Tasks

- ✓ Research **TWO** Great Caribbean Leaders
- ✓ Learn more about the accomplishments of these two Caribbean Leaders and the benefits of their contributions to society.
- ✓ Evaluate your own potential for greatness

Preamble

What makes a person Great! Is it money? Could it be looks? Can a poor person be great? Hitting a ball? Screaming in a microphone? What *does* make a person great?

The words to a once popular song said, "Everybody's searching for a hero. People need someone to look up to." What does it take to become a hero, or are heroes born?

In the spring of 2009, people all over the world became transfixed by a video clip of a woman singing. In just three weeks, the video of the woman's performance was downloaded more than 180 million times. It wasn't a starlet singing her latest Top 40 hit, though, but rather 48-year-old unknown amateur, belting out a 29-year-old song (I Dreamed a Dream) from a Broadway musical. No one expected much of Susan Boyle when she stepped onto the stage of the reality television show "Britain's Got Talent". Subconsciously or not, we expect success from young and beautiful people. We delight in child prodigies and their accomplishments, such as Mozart composing at 5 and Bobby Fischer winning chess championships at the age of 13. Also, when someone has success, we're inclined to say that this is something he or she was born to do; after all, Tiger Woods picked up his first golf club when he was 2.

The Caribbean has produced some very outstanding leaders in various fields and occupations. We continue to be proud of the accomplishments of our Caribbean Greats. Our society continues to benefit from the contributions of these heroes. These individuals have made significant contributions in Science and Technology, Medicine, Sports, Politics, Entertainment, Literature, and the Environment.

Let us acknowledge their accomplishments by learning more about them and the benefits of their contributions to society, and, in turn, perhaps learn how we too can achieve **greatness**.

From Sherwood Content in Trelawny, Jamaica, "To The World", is the story of arguably the world greatest sprinter, Dr. The Hon. Usain St. Leo Bolt, OJ, CD. Usain Bolt was born under humble circumstances to parents Wellesley and Jenifer Bolt. Bolt never had riches, but what he had was a dream…..determination and dedication. Today, this great Caribbean man is known across the world for his exploits on the track. He is currently the fastest man ever to grace the world, and has several accolades which are worthy of emulation. The key characteristic of Bolt is his drive for continued excellence, to make the best, better and to make the impossible, possible. Prodigy and sportsman par excellence are just a few words to describe Usain St. Leo Bolt.

Another great Caribbean leader is Sir Grantley Adams of Barbados. Some describe him as a political legend, the father of the nation, and also as visionary. Sir Adams served as the first Prime Minister of the West Indies Federation. He rose to prominence as he fought for political liberation, and advancing the cause of the workers and the exploited masses of Barbados. Today, he is regarded as one of the regions greatest political leaders. All Sir Grantley Adams had was a vision, one which he believed, and he went beyond the call of duty to achieve. The end result is the great nation, Barbados, which you now see today.

RAISING LEADERS IN THE CLASSROOM

Name of Teacher: _____
Name of Student: _____

a. In pairs, select TWO Caribbean Greats and conduct an internet search. You will have to read through the information first and then make an informed decision.
b. Design a Power Point or an online Presentation.
c. You will be designing your Presentation by including information based on the topics provided below.
d. Learn as much as possible about each individual.
e. Write down the information first before you begin to enter the information into an online presentation maker.

1. **Date and Place of Birth (you may also include ethnic background** /2

   _____
   _____
   _____
   _____
   _____
   _____
   _____

2. **Family (parents, siblings, spouse, children)** /4

   _____
   _____
   _____
   _____
   _____
   _____

3. A chronological account of his or her life /4

4. Hardships or struggles he or she experienced /4

___

5. Major accomplishments/occupation /4

___

6. How society has benefitted from what he/she is/was best known for? /4

___

7. Cause of death – if applicable

_____
_____
_____
_____
_____
_____
_____

8. Now that you have this information written down, your task now is to choose the presentation maker that you prefer. Be sure to include a picture of your Caribbean Greats, and include other pictures that you think would be appropriate for the presentation, as well as the information gathered above. /11

9. Your Presentation is to be visually appealing. Keep in mind, your target audience (your peers, your teacher, and other teachers) and be sure that it is interesting enough to keep the attention of your audience! /11

Name of Teacher: _____
Name of Student: _____

The Next Caribbean Great – YOU!

The hope is that you have had an opportunity to gain some insight into what has made these Caribbean Greats successful. Maybe you can look at anything these people might have in common. They may have something similar that happened to them in childhood or perhaps they each had a special person influence them. It is also possible that there is something about their personalities that make them successful.

IS THERE A "KEY" TO THEIR SUCCESS?

People who are successful and fulfilled, share common characteristics. They believe their success has very little to do with what they have and everything to do with who they are. They hold an ideal about the kind of person they want to be.

The quality of your life is based on the manner in which you participate in it. Your participation is based on who you believe you are. You do have beliefs about who you are, even if you have never consciously considered them. We challenge you to examine and expand on the person you are today, and consider a solid vision of the person you dream of becoming.

Successful people are dreamers, and they dream **big** dreams. Their success starts with a vision that is too exciting to remain just a dream.

a. For this next section you will once again be designing this online. This time it will be **ABOUT YOU!!!**

b. Before you begin you must first answer the questions below:

1. **Date and Place of Birth** /2

2. **Family (guardians, parents, siblings, pets, other)** /4

3. Who is your hero and why? (Family member, an entertainer, a sports figure, a teacher-librarian!!!) /3

4. Hardships or struggles you have experienced /4

5. Major accomplishments /4

6. Describe your goal in life and what you hope to do with your life /4

7. Describe one moment of greatness /3

We have all experienced moments of greatness. You may have accomplished something extraordinary. You could have experienced pride as a result of persevering through a difficult situation, or been touched by your ability to contribute to another person's life. These are the times that you were applying the positive traits you naturally possess.

8. One experience in your life that you regret /3

We have all had experiences that filled us with regret. Perhaps you argued with someone you care for, or were impatient with a friend or family member. It is in these moments your negative traits were at play. Once you have defined the building blocks of your behaviour, you are ready to consider the way you would like to show up in your life.

9. **Describe your own code of conduct** /3

We all develop a set of standards to establish how we behave. A Code of Conduct defines how you will behave, and how you want others to see you.

RAISING LEADERS IN THE CLASSROOM

Name of Teacher: _____
Name of Student: _____

Have fun!

Marking Scheme

Part A
    22 marks x2 Great Caribbeans –
    Short Answer Questions   **/44**

Part B
    30 marks =   **/30**

Presentation - Two Caribbean Greats =

                                                                         TOTAL

Name of Teacher: _____
Name of Student: _____

CREATE A BROCHURE for an individual running for one of the positions listed below:

Examples:

President of the Student Council/Union
Member of Local Government
Member of Parliament

Ensure that the leadership qualities, that will enhance the individual's chance of being elected, are highlighted.

OUTLINE should include the following:

- ❖ Educational Background/Portfolio
- ❖ Community Involvement
- ❖ Plans for the organization
- ❖ Achievements
- ❖ Benefits to organization/society
- ❖ Reasons for selecting this individual
- ❖ Platform of a leader
- ❖ Photos
- ❖ Any other relevant details

TOTAL MARKS /50

REFERENCES

Budden, J. (2010). Teaching English: Error Correction. Retrieved from www.teachingenglish.org.uk/language-assistant/teaching-tips/error-correction

Campbell, B. (1996). Multiple Intelligences in the Classroom. Retrieved from http://www.context.org/iclib/ic27/campbell/

Lukacs, K. (2014). Beyond Teacher Leadership: Teachers as the agents of change in schools. Retrieved from www.academia.edu/3473560/Beyond_teacher_leadersip_Teachers_as_the_agents_of_change_in_schools

ABOUT THE AUTHOR

HEATHER THANE is an educational consultant, master teacher, curriculum developer, and motivational speaker, who resides and teaches in Canada. She is a published author of three books, "Unlock your Greatness Leadership Coaches' Manual", "I am a Leader Coaches' Manual", "Teaching Educators to Raise Leaders: 3D Leadership Concept", and has edited many books. She is certified by the Ontario College of Teachers and holds a Master of Science Degree in Education and a Bachelor of Science Degree in Accounting. Heather has taught teachers in Bachelor of Education programs in the Caribbean, and has a wealth of solid teaching experiences at the elementary school, high school, college, and university levels. She has also spent significant time in coordinating and developing curricula for national youth programs, community college, and teacher education programs.

Heather, with a 25-year success in education, has relied on purposeful strategies used to motivate, 'win over', shape, and engage learners. Indeed, what began as a passion for teaching has through the years of inspiration, consolidated into a **3D Approach to Education and Leadership.**

www.ingramcontent.com/pod-product-compliance
Lightning Source LLC
Chambersburg PA
CBHW071222160426
43196CB00012B/2379